RANDOM HOUSE

TREASURY OF BEST-LOVED CHILDREN'S POEMS

Edited by Patricia S. Klein

RANDOM HOUSE
REFERNCE

New York   Toronto   London   Sydney   Auckland

Visit the Random House Web site: www.randomhouse.com

Library of Congress Cataloging-in-Publication Data is available.

First Edition
0 9 8 7 6 5 4 3 2 1

ISBN-13: 978-0-375-72145-8
ISBN-10: 0-375-72145-2

Printed in China

To my lovely niece Emma,
who loves poetry.

Poetry

What is poetry? Who knows?
Not the rose, but the scent of the rose;
Not the sky, but the light in the sky;
Not the fly, but the gleam of the fly;
Not the sea, but the sound of the sea;
Not myself, but what makes me
See, hear, and feel something that prose
Cannot: and what it is, who knows?

—*Eleanor Farjeon*

CONTENTS

1   Me and My Family

21   Come Out and Play!

43   I'm Hungry!

57   Some Good Advice

69   Silly, Silly, Silly!

85   Read Me a Story, Please

105   Grand Adventures

123   Things That Go Bump in the Night

139   Lions and Tigers and Bears—and More

155   Our Great, Wide, Beautiful, Wonderful World

173   Wind and Rain and Snow

189   Sun and Moon and Stars

207   Bedtime Blessings

229   PERMISSIONS ACKNOWLEDGMENTS

235   INDEX OF AUTHORS

237   INDEX OF TITLES

240   INDEX OF FIRST LINES

ME AND MY FAMILY

Afternoon on a Hill

I will be the gladdest thing
   Under the sun!
I will touch a hundred flowers
   And not pick one.

I will look at cliffs and clouds
   With quiet eyes,
Watch the wind bow down the grass,
   And the grass rise.

And when lights begin to show
   Up from the town,
I will mark which must be mine,
   And then start down!

—*Edna St. Vincent Millay*

Measure Me, Sky!

Measure me, sky!
  Tell me I reach by a song
Nearer the stars;
  I have been little so long!

Weigh me, high wind!
  What will your wild scales record?
Profit of pain,
  Joy by the weight of a word!

Horizon, reach out!
  Catch at my hands, stretch me taut,
Rim of the world;
  Widen my eyes by a thought!

Sky, be my depth,
  Wind, be my width and my height,
World, my heart's span;
  Loneliness, wings for my flight!

—*Leonora Speyer*

Myself

As I walked by myself,
And talked to myself,
Myself said unto me:
"Look to thyself,
Take care of thyself,
For nobody cares for thee."

I answered myself,
And said to myself
In the self-same repartee:
"Look to thyself,
Or not look to thyself,
The self-same thing will be."

Me

As long as I live
I shall always be
My Self—and no other,
Just me.

Like a tree—
Willow, elder,
Aspen, thorn,
Or cypress forlorn.

Like a flower,
For its hour—
Primrose, or pink,
Or a violet—
Sunned by the sun,
And with dewdrops wet.

Always just me.
Till the day come on
When I leave this body,
It's all then done,
And the spirit within it
Is gone.

—*Walter de la Mare*

My Shadow

I have a little shadow that goes in and out
    with me,
And what can be the use of him is more than I
    can see.
He is very, very like me from the heels up to
    the head;
And I see him jump before me, when I jump
    into my bed.

The funniest thing about him is the way he
    likes to grow—
Not at all like proper children, which is always
    very slow;
For he sometimes shoots up taller like an India-
    rubber ball,
And he sometimes gets so little that there's
    none of him at all.

He hasn't got a notion of how children ought
   to play,
And can only make a fool of me in every sort
   of way.
He stays so close beside me, he's a coward you
   can see;
I'd think shame to stick to nursie as that shadow
   sticks to me!

One morning, very early, before the sun was up,
I rose and found the shining dew on every
   buttercup;
But my lazy little shadow, like an arrant
   sleepy-head,
Had stayed at home behind me and was fast
   asleep in bed.

—*Robert Louis Stevenson*

"I'm nobody! Who are you?"

I'm nobody! Who are you?
Are you nobody too?
Then there's a pair of us.
Don't tell—they'd banish us, you know.

How dreary to be somebody!
How public—like a frog—
To tell your name the livelong June
To an admiring bog.

—*Emily Dickinson*

The Wrong Start

I got up this morning and meant to be good,
But things didn't happen the way that they
   should.

   I lost my toothbrush,
      I slammed the door,
   I dropped an egg
      On the kitchen floor,
   I spilled some sugar
      And after that
   I tried to hurry
      And tripped on the cat.

Things may get better. I don't know when.
I think I'll go back and start over again.

—*Marchette Chute*

Mr. Nobody

I know a funny little man,
   As quiet as a mouse,
Who does the mischief that is done
   In everybody's house!
There's no one ever sees his face,
   And yet we all agree
That every plate we break was cracked
   By Mr. Nobody.

'Tis he who always tears our books,
   Who leaves the door ajar;
He pulls the buttons from our shirts,
   And scatters pins afar;
That squeaking door will always squeak,
   For, prithee, don't you see,
We leave the oiling to be done
   By Mr. Nobody.

He puts damp wood upon the fire,
    That kettles cannot boil;
His are the feet that bring in the mud,
    And all the carpets soil.
The papers always are mislaid,
    Who had them last but he?
There's not one tosses them about
    But Mr. Nobody.

The finger-marks upon the door
    By none of us are made;
We never leave the blinds unclosed,
    To let the curtains fade;
The ink we never spill, the boots
    That lying around you see
Are not our boots; they all belong
    To Mr. Nobody!

Two People

She reads the paper,
while he turns on TV;
she likes the mountains,
he craves the sea.

He'd rather drive,
she'll take the plane;
he waits for sunshine;
she walks in the rain.

He gulps down cold drinks,
she sips at hot;
he asks, "Why go?"
She asks, "Why not?"

In just about everything
they disagree,
but they love one another
and they both love me.

—*Eve Merriam*

Human Affection

Mother, I love you so.
Said the child, I love you more than I know.
She laid her head on her mother's arm,
And the love between them kept them warm.

—*Stevie Smith*

Daddy Fell into the Pond

Everyone grumbled. The sky was gray.
We had nothing to do and nothing to say.
We were nearing the end of a dismal day,
And there seemed to be nothing beyond,
   THEN
   Daddy fell into the pond!

And everyone's face grew merry and bright,
And Timothy danced for sheer delight.
"Give me the camera, quick, oh quick!
He's crawling out of the duckweed!" *Click!*

Then the gardener suddenly slapped his knee,
And doubled up, shaking silently,
And the ducks all quacked as if they were daft
And it sounded as if the old drake laughed.

Oh, there wasn't a thing that didn't respond
   WHEN
   Daddy fell into the pond!

—*Alfred Noyes*

Two in Bed

When my brother Tommy
Sleeps in bed with me,
He doubles up
and makes
himself
exactly
like
a
V

And 'cause the bed is not so wide,
A part of him is on my side.

—*A. B. Ross*

Little Brother's Secret

When my birthday was coming
Little Brother had a secret
He kept it for days and days
And just hummed a little tune when I asked him.
But one night it rained
And I woke up and heard him crying.
Then he told me
"I planted two lumps of sugar in your garden
Because you love it so frightfully
I thought there would be a whole sugar tree for
  your birthday
And now it will all be melted."
O, the darling!

—*Katherine Mansfield*

Love Between Brothers and Sisters

Whatever brawls disturb the street,
   There should be peace at home:
Where sisters dwell and brothers meet,
   Quarrels should never come.

Birds in their little nests agree;
   And 'tis a shameful sight,
When children of one family
   Fall out and chide and fight.

—*Isaac Watts*

Manners

I have an uncle I don't like,
   An aunt I cannot bear:
She chucks me underneath the chin,
   He ruffles up my hair.

Another uncle I adore,
   Another aunty, too:
She shakes me kindly by the hand,
   He says, "How do you do?"

—*Mariana Griswold Van Rensselaer*

COME OUT AND PLAY! ⤳

Come Out to Play

Girls and boys, come out to play,
The moon doth shine as bright as day;
Leave your supper and leave your sleep,
And come with your playfellows into the street.
Come with a whoop, come with a call,
Come with a good will or not at all.
Up the ladder and down the wall,
A half-penny roll will serve·us all.
You find milk, and I'll find flour,
And we'll have a pudding in half an hour.

The Pasture

I'm going out to clean the pasture spring;
I'll only stop to rake the leaves away
(And wait to watch the water clear, I may):
I sha'n't be long.—You come too.

I'm going out to fetch the little calf
That's standing by the mother. It's so young,
It totters when she licks it with her tongue.
I sha'n't be gone long.—You come too.

—*Robert Frost*

Frolic

The children were shouting together
And racing along the sands,
A glimmer of dancing shadows,
A dovelike flutter of hands.

The stars were shouting in heaven,
The sun was chasing the moon:
The game was the same as the children's,
They danced to the self-same tune.

The whole of the world was merry,
One joy from the vale to the height,
Where the blue woods of twilight encircled
The lovely lawns of the light.

—*George William ("Æ") Russell*

Ring-a-Ring

Ring-a-ring of little boys.
  Ring-a-ring of girls;
All around—all around,
  Twists and twirls.

You are merry children.
  "Yes, we are."
Where do you come from?
  "Not very far.

"We live in the mountain,
  We live in the tree;
And I live in the river bed,
  And you won't catch me!"

  –Kate Greenaway

A Song of Sixpence

Sing a song of sixpence,
   A pocket full of rye;
Four and twenty blackbirds
   Baked in a pie;

When the pie was opened,
   The birds began to sing;
Wasn't that a dainty dish
   To set before the king?

The king was in his counting-house
   Counting out his money;
The queen was in the parlor
   Eating bread and honey;

The maid was in the garden
   Hanging out the clothes,
Along came a blackbird
   And nipped off her nose.

One, two,
Buckle my shoe;
Three, four,
Shut the door;
Five, six,
Pick up sticks;
Seven, eight,
Lay them straight;
Nine, ten,
A big fat hen;
Eleven, twelve,
Who will delve?
Thirteen, fourteen,
Maids a-courting;
Fifteen, sixteen,
Maids a-kissing;
Seventeen, eighteen,
Maids a-waiting;
Nineteen, twenty,
My stomach's empty.

This little piggy went to market;
This little piggy stayed home;
This little piggy had roast beef;
This little piggy had none;
And this little piggy cried, "Wee! Wee! Wee!"
All the way home.

*   *   *

There was a crooked man,
    And he walked a crooked mile;
He found a crooked sixpence
    Beside a crooked stile;
He bought a crooked cat
    And it caught a crooked mouse
And they both lived together
    In a wee crooked house.

I Meant to Do My Work Today

I meant to do my work today—
    But a brown bird sang in the apple tree,
And a butterfly flitted across the field,
    And all the leaves were calling me.

And the wind went sighing over the land,
    Tossing the grasses to and fro,
And a rainbow held out its shining hand—
    So what could I do but laugh and go?

—*Richard LeGallienne*

A Good Play

We built a ship upon the stairs,
All made of the back-bedroom chairs,
And filled it full of sofa pillows
To go a-sailing on the billows.

We took a saw and several nails,
And water in the nursery pails;
And Tom said, "Let us also take
An apple and a slice of cake";—
Which was enough for Tom and me
To go a-sailing on, till tea.

We sailed along for days and days,
And had the very best of plays;
But Tom fell out and hurt his knee,
So there was no one left but me.

—*Robert Louis Stevenson*

A Boy's Song

Where the pools are bright and deep,
Where the grey trout lies asleep,
Up the river and o'er the lea,
That's the way for Billy and me.

Where the blackbird sings the latest,
Where the hawthorn blooms the sweetest,
Where the nestlings chirp and flee,
That's the way for Billy and me.

Where the mowers mow the cleanest,
Where the hay lies thick and greenest,
There to track the homeward bee,
That's the way for Billy and me.

Where the hazel bank is steepest,
Where the shadow falls the deepest,
Where the clustering nuts fall free,
That's the way for Billy and me.

Why the boys should drive away
Little sweet maidens from the play,
Or love to banter and fight so well,
That's the thing I never could tell.

But this I know, I love to play,
Through the meadow, among the hay;
Up the water and o'er the lea,
That's the way for Billy and me.

—*James Hogg*

Bicycling Song

With lifted feet, hands still,
I am poised, and down the hill
Dart, with heedful mind;
The air goes by in a wind.

Swifter and yet more swift,
Till the heart with a mighty lift
Makes the lungs laugh, the throat cry:—
'O bird, see; see, bird, I fly.

'Is this, is this your joy?
O bird, then I, though a boy
For a golden moment share
Your feathery life in air!'

Say, heart, is there aught like this
In a world that is full of bliss?
'Tis more than skating, bound
Steel-shod to the level ground.

Speed slackens now, I float
Awhile in my airy boat;
Till, when the wheels scarce crawl,
My feet to the treadles fall.

Alas, that the longest hill
Must end in a vale; but still,
Who climbs with toil, wheresoe'er,
Shall find wings waiting there.

—*Henry Charles Beeching*

Hiding

I'm hiding, I'm hiding,
  And no one knows where;
For all they can see is my
  Toes and my hair.

And I just heard my father
  Say to my mother—
"But, darling, he must be
  Somewhere or other;

Have you looked in the inkwell?"
  And Mother said, "Where?"
"In the *inkwell*," said Father. But
  I was not there.

Then "Wait!" cried my mother—
  "I think that I see
Him under the carpet." But
  It was not me.

"Inside the mirror's
   A pretty good place,"
Said father and looked, but saw
   Only his face.

"We've hunted," sighed Mother,
   "As hard as we could
And I *am* so afraid that we've
   Lost him for good."

Then I laughed out aloud
   And I wiggled my toes
And Father said—"Look, dear,
   I wonder if those

"Toes could be Benny's?
   There are ten of them, see?"
And they *were* so surprised to find
   Out it was me!

—*Dorothy Aldis*

Mud!

Mud is very nice to feel
All squishy-squash between the toes!
I'd rather wade in wiggly mud
Than smell a yellow rose.

Nobody else but the rosebush knows
How nice mud feels
Between the toes.

—*Polly Chase Boyden*

A Swing Song

   Swing, swing,
   Sing, sing,
Here! my throne and I am a king!
   Swing, sing
   Swing, sing,
Farewell, earth, for I'm on the wing!

   Low, high,
   Here I fly,
Like a bird through sunny sky;
   Free, free,
   Over the lea,
Over the mountain, over the sea!

   Up, down,
   Up and down,
Which is the way to London Town?
   Where? Where?
   Up in the air,
Close your eyes and now you are there!

Soon, soon,
Afternoon,
Over the sunset, over the moon;
Far, far,
Over all bar,
Sweeping on from start to star!

No, no
Low, low,
Sweeping daisies with my toe.
Slow, slow,
To and fro,
Slow—slow—slow—slow.

—*William Allingham*

The Swing

How do you like to go up in a swing,
  Up in the air so blue?
Oh, I do think it the pleasantest thing
  Ever a child can do!

Up in the air and over the wall,
  Till I can see so wide,
River and trees and cattle and all
  Over the countryside—

Till I look down on the garden green,
  Down on the roof so brown—
Up in the air I go flying again,
  Up in the air and down!

—*Robert Louis Stevenson*

My Little Doll, from *The Water-Babies*

I once had a sweet little doll, dears,
  The prettiest doll in the world;
Her cheeks were so red and so white, dears,
  And her hair was so charmingly curled.
But I lost my poor little doll, dears,
  As I played on the heath one day;
And I cried for her more than a week, dears,
  But I never could find where she lay.

I found my poor little doll, dears,
  As I played on the heath one day;
Folks say she is terribly changed, dears,
  For her paint is all washed away,
And her arm trodden off by the cows, dears,
  And her hair not the least bit curled;
Yet for old time's sake, she is still, dears,
  The prettiest doll in the world.

—*Charles Kingsley*

Self-Control

My dolly would not play with me.
She simply stared
Her silly stare.
It made me *wild*
To pull her hair.

I kissed her *very quietly*
And walked outdoors and kicked a tree.

—*Polly Chase Boyden*

I'M HUNGRY!

Animal Crackers

Animal crackers, and cocoa to drink,
That is the finest of suppers, I think;
When I'm grown up and can have what I please
I think I shall always insist upon these.

What do *you* choose when you're offered a treat?
When Mother says, "What would you like best
    to eat?"
Is it waffles and syrup, or cinnamon toast?
It's cocoa and animals that *I* love most!

The kitchen's the cosiest place that I know:
The kettle is singing, the stove is aglow,
And there in the twilight, how jolly to see
The cocoa and animals waiting for me.

Daddy and Mother dine later in state,
With Mary to cook for them, Susan to wait;
But they don't have nearly as much fun as I
Who eat in the kitchen with Nurse standing by;
And Daddy once said, he would like to be me
Having cocoa and animals once more for tea!

—*Christopher Darlington Morley*

The Cupboard

I know a little cupboard,
 With a teeny tiny key,
And there's a jar of Lollipops
 For me, me, me.

It has a little shelf, my dear,
 As dark as dark can be,
And there's a dish of Banbury Cakes
 For me, me, me.

I have a small fat grandmamma,
 With a very slippery knee,
And she's Keeper of the Cupboard,
 With the key, key, key.

And when I'm very good, my dear,
 As good as good can be,
There's Banbury Cakes, and Lollipops
 For me, me, me.

—*Walter de la Mare*

Turtle Soup

Beautiful Soup, so rich and green,
Waiting in a hot tureen!
Who for such dainties would not stoop?
Soup of the evening, beautiful Soup!
Soup of the evening, beautiful Soup!
   Beau—ootiful Soo—oop!
   Beau—ootiful Soo—oop!
Soo—oop of the e—e—evening,
   Beautiful, beautiful Soup!

Beautiful Soup! Who cares for fish,
Game, or any other dish?
Who would not give all else for two
Pennyworth only of beautiful Soup?
Pennyworth only of beautiful Soup?
   Beau—ootiful Soo—oop!
   Beau— ootiful Soo—oop!
Soo—oop of the e—e—evening,
   Beautiful, beauti—FUL SOUP!

—*Lewis Carroll*

Millions of Strawberries

Marcia and I went over the curve,
Eating our way down
Jewels of strawberries we didn't deserve,
Eating our way down.
Till our hands were sticky, and our lips painted,
And over us the hot day fainted,
And we saw snakes,
And got scratched,
And a lust came over us for the red unmatched
Small buds of berries,
Till we lay down—
Eating our way down—
And rolled in the berries like two little dogs,
Rolled
In the late gold.
And gnats hummed,
And it was cold,
And home we went, home without a berry,
Painted red and brown,
Eating our way down.

—*Genevieve Taggard*

The Crust of Bread

I must not throw upon the floor
   The crust I cannot eat;
For many hungry little ones
   Would think it quite a treat.

My parents labor very hard
   To get me wholesome food;
Then I must never waste a bit
   That would do others good.

For wilful waste makes woeful want,
   And I may live to say,
Oh! how I wish I had the bread
   That once I threw away!

Table Graces

Some hae meat, and canna eat,
And some wad eat that want it,
But we hae meat and we can eat
And sae the Lord be thankit.

—*Robert Burns*

*   *   *

Be present at our table, Lord,
Be here and everywhere adored
Thy creatures bless, and grant that we
May feast in Paradise with Thee.

—*John Wesley*

Peter Piper picked a peck of pickled peppers;
A peck of pickled peppers Peter Piper picked.
If Peter Piper picked a peck of pickled peppers,
Where's the peck of pickled peppers Peter
Piper picked?

*   *   *

Betty Botter bought some butter,
But she said, the butter's bitter;
If I put it in my batter
It will make my batter bitter,
But a bit of better butter,
That would make my batter better.
So she bought a bit of butter
Better than her bitter butter,
And she put it in her batter
And the batter was not bitter.
So t'was better Betty Botter
Bought a bit of better butter.

There was a young lady of Lynn,
Who was so uncommonly thin
   That when she essayed
   To drink lemonade,
She slipped through the straw and fell in.

*   *   *

An epicure, dining at Crewe,
Found quite a large mouse in his stew.
   Said the waiter, "Don't shout
   And wave it about
Or the rest will be wanting one, too."

A peanut sat on a railroad track,
His heart was all a-flutter;
The five-fifteen came rushing by—
Toot! toot! peanut butter!

*   *   *

I eat my peas with honey;
I've done it all my life.
It makes the peas taste funny,
But it keeps them on the knife.

The Goops

The Goops they lick their fingers,
   And the Goops they lick their knives;
They spill their broth on the tablecloth—
   Oh, they lead disgusting lives!
The Goops they talk while eating,
   And loud and fast they chew;
And that is why I'm glad that I
   Am not a Goop—are you?

—*Frank Gelett Burgess*

*   *   *

Whole Duty of Children

A child should always say what's true
And speak when he is spoken to,
And behave mannerly at table;
At least as far as he is able.

—*Robert Louis Stevenson*

SOME GOOD ADVICE ⌒

Rules for the Road

Stand straight:
Step firmly, throw your weight:
The heaven is high above your head,
The good gray road is faithful to your tread.

Be strong:
Sing to your heart a battle song:
Though hidden foemen lie in wait,
Something is in you that can smile at Fate.

Press through:
Nothing can harm if you are true.
And when the night comes, rest:
The earth is friendly as a mother's breast.

—*Edwin Markham*

Politeness

If people ask me,
I always tell them:
"Quite well, thank you, I'm very glad to say."
If people ask me,
I always answer,
"Quite well, thank you, how are you to-day?"
I always answer,
I always tell them,
If they ask me
Politely. . . . .
BUT SOMETIMES
  I wish
    That they wouldn't.

— *A. A. Milne*

Let others share your toys, my son,
Do not insist on *all* the fun.
For if you don it's certain that
You'll grow to be an adult brat.

—*Edward Anthony*

*   *   *

   Don't shirk
   Your work
For the sake of a dream;
   A fish
   In the dish
Is worth ten in the stream.

*   *   *

When in danger,
When in doubt,
Run in circles,
Scream and shout.

Chartless

I never saw a moor,
I never saw the sea;
Yet now I know how the heather looks,
And what a wave must be.

I never spoke with God,
Nor visited in Heaven;
Yet certain am I of the spot
As if the chart were given.

— *Emily Dickinson*

Little Things

Little drops of water,
  Little grains of sand,
Make the mighty ocean
  And the pleasant land.

So the little moments,
  Humble though they be,
Make the mighty ages
  Of eternity.

So our little errors
  Lead the soul away
From the path of virtue,
  Far in sin to stray.

Little deeds of kindness,
  Little words of love,
Help to make earth happy
  Like the heaven above.

—*Julia Fletcher Carney*

Barter

Life has loveliness to sell,
   All beautiful and splendid things,
Blue waves whitened on a cliff,
   Soaring fire that sways and sings,
And children's faces looking up
Holding wonder like a cup.

Life has loveliness to sell,
   Music like a curve of gold,
Scent of pine trees in the rain,
   Eyes that love you, arms that hold,
And for your spirit's still delight,
Holy thoughts that star the night.

Spend all you have for loveliness,
   Buy it and never count the cost;
For one white singing hour of peace
   Count many a year of strife well lost,
And for a breath of ecstasy
Give all you have been, or could be.

—*Sara Teasdale*

Simple Gifts

'Tis the gift to be simple,
'Tis the gift to be free,
'Tis the gift to come down where we ought to be,
And when we find ourselves in the place
   just right,
It will be in the valley of love and delight.

When true simplicity is gained,
to bow and to bend, we will not be ashamed
To turn, turn, will be our delight,
'Til by turning, turning, we come round right.

—*Joseph Brackett Jr.*

If I Can Stop One Heart From Breaking

If I can stop one Heart from breaking
I shall not live in vain
If I can ease one Life the Aching
Or cool one Pain

Or help one fainting Robin
Unto his Nest again
I shall not live in Vain.

—*Emily Dickinson*

If

If you can keep your head when all about you
    Are losing theirs and blaming it on you;
If you can trust yourself when all men doubt you,
    But make allowance for their doubting too;
If you can wait and not be tired by waiting,
    Or, being lied about, don't deal in lies,
Or, being hated, don't give way to hating,
    And yet don't look too good, nor talk too wise;

If you can dream—and not make dreams your
      master;
If you can think—and not make thoughts
      your aim;
If you can meet with triumph and disaster
    And treat those two impostors just the same;
If you can bear to hear the truth you've spoken
    Twisted by knaves to make a trap for fools,
Or watch the things you gave your life to broken,
    And stoop and build 'em up with wornout
      tools;

If you can make one heap of all your winnings
    And risk it on one turn of pitch-and-toss,
And lose, and start again at your beginnings
    And never breathe a word about your loss;
If you can force your heart and nerve and sinew
    To serve your turn long after they are gone,
And so hold on when there is nothing in you
    Except the Will which says to them: "Hold on";

If you can talk with crowds and keep your virtue,
    Or walk with kings—nor lose the common
        touch;
If neither foes nor loving friends can hurt you;
    If all men count with you, but none too much;
If you can fill the unforgiving minute
    With sixty seconds' worth of distance run—
Yours is the Earth and everything that's in it,
    And—which is more—you'll be a Man, my
        son!

—*Rudyard Kipling*

Hold Fast to Dreams

Hold fast to dreams
For if dreams die
Life is a broken-winged bird
That cannot fly.

Hold fast to dreams
For when dreams go
Life is a barren field
Frozen with snow.

—Langston Hughes

SILLY, SILLY, SILLY!

Jabberwocky

'Twas brillig, and the slithy toves
    Did gyre and gimble in the wabe:
All mimsy were the borogoves,
    And the mome raths outgrabe.

"Beware the Jabberwock, my son!
    The jaws that bite, the claws that catch!
Beware the Jubjub bird, and shun
    The frumious Bandersnatch!"

He took his vorpal sword in hand:
    Long time the manxome foe he sought—
So rested he by the Tumtum tree,
    And stood awhile in thought.

And, as in uffish thought he stood,
    The Jabberwock, with eyes of flame,
Came whiffling through the tulgey wood,
    And burbled as it came!

One, two! One, two! And through and through
  The vorpal blade went snicker-snack!
He left it dead, and with its head
  He went galumphing back.

"And hast thou slain the Jabberwock?
  Come to my arms, my beamish boy!
O frabjous day! Callooh! Callay!"
  He chortled in his joy.

"'Twas brillig, and the slithy toves
  Did gyre and gimble in the wabe:
All mimsy were the borogoves,
  And the mome raths outgrabe.

—*Lewis Carroll*

Eletelephony

Once there was an elephant,
Who tried to use the telephant—
No! no! I mean an elephone
Who tried to use the telephone—
(Dear me! I am not certain quite
That even now I've got it right.)

Howe'er it was, he got his trunk
Entangled in the telephunk;
The more he tried to get it free,
The louder buzzed the telephee—
(I fear I'd better drop the song
Of elephop and telephong!)

—*Laura Elizabeth Richards*

There was an Old Man with a beard,
Who said, "It is just as I feared!—
  Two Owls and a Hen,
  Four Larks and a Wren,
Have all built their nests in my beard!"

—*Edward Lear*

*   *   *

A tutor who tooted the flute
Tried to tutor two tooters to toot,
  Said the two to the tutor,
  "Is it harder to toot or
To tutor two tooters to toot?"

*   *   *

There was a young lady named Bright
Whose speed was far faster than light;
   She set out one day,
   In the relative way
And returned on the previous night.

A flea and a fly in a flue
Were imprisoned, so what could they do?
  Said the fly, "Let us flee!"
  "Let us fly!" said the flea,
So they flew through a flaw in the flue.

Fuzzy Wuzzy was a bear,
Fuzzy Wuzzy had no hair,
Fuzzy Wuzzy wasn't fuzzy,
was he?

* * *

How much wood would a woodchuck chuck
If a woodchuck could chuck wood?
He would chuck what wood a woodchuck
    would chuck,
If a woodchuck could chuck wood.

The Purple Cow

I never saw a Purple Cow,
  I never hope to see one;
But I can tell you, anyhow,
  I'd rather see than be one.

—*Frank Gelett Burgess*

*   *   *

As I was standing in the street,
  As quiet as could be,
A great big ugly man came up
  And tied his horse to me!

Higglety, Pigglety, Pop!

Higglety, pigglety, pop!
The dog has ate the mop;
The pig's in a hurry,
The cat's in a flurry,
Higglety, pigglety, pop!

—*Samuel Griswold Goodrich*

Song of the Pop-Bottlers

Pop bottles pop-bottles
In pop shops;
The pop-bottles Pop bottles
Poor Pop drops.

When Pop drops pop-bottles,
Pop-bottles plop!
Pop bottle-tops topple!
Pop mops slop!

Stop! Pop'll drop bottle!
Stop, Pop, stop!
When Pop bottles pop-bottles,
Pop-bottles pop!

—*Morris Bishop*

The Gardener's Song

He thought he saw an Elephant,
   That practised on a fife:
He looked again, and found it was
   A letter from his wife.
"At length I realise," he said,
   "The bitterness of Life!"

He thought he saw a Buffalo
   Upon the chimney-piece:
He looked again, and found it was
   His Sister's Husband's Niece.
"Unless you leave this house," he said,
   "I'll send for the Police!"

He thought he saw a Rattlesnake
   That questioned him in Greek:
He looked again, and found it was
   The Middle of Next Week.
"The one thing I regret," he said,
   "Is that it cannot speak!"

He thought he saw a Banker's Clerk
  Descending from the bus:
He looked again, and found it was
  A Hippopotamus.
"If this should stay to dine," he said,
  "There won't be much for us!"

He thought he saw a Kangaroo
  That worked a coffee-mill:
He looked again, and found it was
  A Vegetable-Pill.
"Were I to swallow this," he said,
  "I should be very ill!"

He thought he saw a Coach-and-Four
  That stood beside his bed:
He looked again, and found it was
  A Bear without a Head.
"Poor thing," he said, "poor silly thing!
  It's waiting to be fed!"

He thought he saw an Albatross
   That fluttered round the lamp:
He looked again, and found it was
   A Penny-Postage-Stamp.
"You'd best be getting home," he said:
   "The nights are very damp!"

He thought he saw a Garden-Door
   That opened with a key:
He looked again, and found it was
   A double Rule of Three:
"And all its mystery," he said,
   "Is clear as day to me!"

He thought he saw a Argument
   That proved he was the Pope:
He looked again, and found it was
   A Bar of Mottled Soap.
"A fact so dread," he faintly said,
   "Extinguishes all hope!"

—*Lewis Carroll*

Bad Report—Good Manners

My daddy said, "My son, my son,
This school report is bad."
I said, "I did my best I did,
My dad my dad my dad."

"Explain, my son, my son," he said,
"Why the *bottom* of the class?"
"I stood aside, my dad my dad,
To let the others pass."

—*Spike Milligan*

Routine

No matter what we are and who,
some duties everyone must do:

A Poet puts aside his wreath
To wash his face and brush his teeth,

And even Earls
Must comb their curls,

And even Kings
Have underthings.

—*Arthur Guiterman*

READ ME A STORY, PLEASE

A Book

There is no frigate like a book
   To take us lands away,
Nor any coursers like a page
   Of prancing poetry.

This traverse may the poorest take.
   Without oppress of toll;
How frugal is the chariot
   That bears a human soul!

—*Emily Dickinson*

To Any Reader

As from the house your mother sees
You playing round the garden trees,
So you may see, if you will look
Through the windows of this book,
Another child, far, far away,
And in another garden, play.
But do not think you can at all,
By knocking on the window, call
That child to hear you. He intent
Is all on his play-business bent.
He does not hear; he will not look,
Nor yet be lured out of his book.
For, long ago, the truth to say,
He has grown up and gone away,
And it is but a child of air
That lingers in the garden there.

—*Robert Louis Stevenson*

When Mother Reads Aloud

When Mother reads aloud, the past
   Seems real as every day;
I hear the tramp of armies vast,
I see the spears and lances cast,
   I join the trilling fray;
Brave knights and ladies fair and proud
I meet when Mother reads aloud.

When Mother reads aloud, far lands
   Seem very near and true;
I cross the desert's gleaming sands,
Or hunt the jungle's prowling bands,
   Or sail the ocean blue.
Far heights, whose peaks the cold mists shroud,
I scale, when Mother reads aloud.

When Mother reads aloud, I long
   For noble deeds to do—
To help the right, redress the wrong;
It seems so easy to be strong,
   So simple to be true.
Oh, thick and fast the visions crowd
My eyes, when Mother reads aloud.

The Land of Story-Books

At evening when the lamp is lit,
Around the fire my parents sit;
They sit at home and talk and sing,
And do not play at anything.

Now, with my little gun, I crawl
All in the dark along the wall,
And follow round the forest track
Away behind the sofa back.

There, in the night, where none can spy,
All in my hunter's camp I lie,
And play at books that I have read
Till it is time to go to bed.

These are the hills, these are the woods,
These are my starry solitudes;
And there the river by whose brink
The roaring lions come to drink.

I see the others far away.
As if in firelit camp they lay,
And I, like to an Indian scout,
Around their party prowled about.

So, when my nurse comes in for me,
Home I return across the sea,
And go to bed with backward looks
At my dear Land of Story-Books.

—*Robert Louis Stevenson*

The Duel

The gingham dog and the calico cat
   Side by side on the table sat;
   'Twas half-past twelve, and (what do you
     think!)
Nor one nor t'other had slept a wink!
   The old Dutch clock and the Chinese plate
   Appeared to know as sure as fate
There was going to be a terrible spat.
     (I wasn't there; I simply state
     What was told to me by the Chinese plate!)

The gingham dog went "bow-wow-wow!"
And the calico cat replied "me-ow!"
The air was littered, an hour or so,
With bits of gingham and calico,
   While the old Dutch clock in the chimney-
     place
   Up with it hands before its face,
For it always dreaded a family row!
     (Now mind: I'm only telling you
     What the old Dutch clock declares is true!)

The Chinese plate looked very blue,
And wailed, "Oh dear! What shall we do!"
But the gingham dog and the calico cat
Wallowed this way and tumbled that,
Employing every tooth and claw
In the awfullest way you ever saw—
And oh! how the gingham and calico flew!
    (Don't fancy I exaggerate—
    I got my news from the Chinese plate!)

Next morning, where the two had sat
They found no trace of dog or cat;
And some folks think unto this day
That burglars stole the pair away!
    But the truth about the cat and pup
    Is this: they ate each other up!
Now what do you really think of that!
    (The old Dutch clock it told me so,
    And that is how I came to know.)

—*Eugene Field*

The Owl and the Pussy Cat

The Owl and the Pussycat went to sea
   In a beautiful pea-green boat:
They took some honey, and plenty of money
   Wrapped up in a five-pound note.
The Owl looked up to the stars above,
   And sang to a small guitar,
"O lovely Pussy, O Pussy, my love,
   What a beautiful Pussy you are,
           You are,
           You are!
   What a beautiful Pussy you are!"

Pussy said to the Owl, "You elegant fowl,
   How charmingly sweet you sing!
Oh! let us be married; too long we have tarried:
   But what shall we do for a ring?"
They sailed away, for a year and a day,
   To the land where the bong tree grows;

And there in a wood Piggy-wig stood,
　　With a ring at the end of his nose,
　　　　　　His nose,
　　　　　　His nose,
　　With a ring at the end of his nose.

"Dear Pig, are you willing to sell for one shilling
　　Your ring?" said the Piggy "I will."
So they took it away and were married next day
　　By the turkey who lives on the hill.
They dined on mince and slices of quince,
　　Which they ate with a runcible spoon;
And hand in hand, on the edge of the sand,
　　They danced by the light of the moon,
　　　　　　The moon,
　　　　　　The moon,
　　They danced by the light of the moon.

—*Edward Lear*

The Blind Men and the Elephant

It was six men of Indostan
  To learning much inclined,
Who went to see the Elephant
  (Though all of them were blind),
That each by observation
  Might satisfy his mind.

The *First* approached the Elephant,
  And happening to fall
Against his broad and sturdy side,
  At once began to bawl:
"God bless me! but the Elephant
  Is very like a wall!"

The *Second*, feeling of the tusk,
  Cried, "Ho! what have we here
So very round and smooth and sharp?
  To me 'tis mighty clear
This wonder of an Elephant
  Is very like a spear!"

The *Third* approached the animal,
  And happening to take
The squirming trunk within his hands,
  Thus boldly up and spake:
"I see," quoth he, "the Elephant
  Is very like a snake!"

The *Fourth* reached out his eager hand,
  And felt about the knee.
"What most this wondrous beast is like
  Is mighty plain," quoth he;
"'Tis clear enough the Elephant
  Is very like a tree!"

The *Fifth* who chanced to touch the ear,
  Said: "E'en the blindest man
Can tell what this resembles most;
  Deny the fact who can,
This marvel of an Elephant
  Is very like a fan!"

The *Sixth* no sooner had begun
  About the beast to grope,
Than, seizing on the swinging tail
  That fell within his scope,
"I see," quoth he, "the Elephant
  Is very like a rope!"

And so these men of Indostan
  Disputed loud and long,
Each in his own opinion
  Exceeding stiff and strong,
Though each was partly in the right,
  And all were in the wrong!

      Moral
So oft in theologic wars,
  The disputants, I ween,
Rail on in utter ignorance
  Of what each other mean,
And prate about an Elephant
  Not one of them has seen!

—*John Godfrey Saxe*

The Spider and the Fly

"Will you walk into my parlor?" said the Spider
    to the Fly,
"'Tis the prettiest little parlor that ever you
    did spy;
The way into my parlor is up a winding stair,
And I have many curious things to show when
    you are there."
"Oh no, no," said the little Fly, "to ask me is in
    vain;
For who goes up your winding stair can ne'er
    come down again."

"I'm sure you must be weary, dear, with soaring
    up so high;
Will you rest upon my little bed?" said the Spider
    to the Fly.
"There are pretty curtains drawn around, the
    sheets are fine and thin;
And if you like to rest awhile, I'll snugly tuck
    you in!"

"Oh no, no," said the little Fly, "for I've often
  heard it said
They never, never wake again, who sleep upon
  your bed!"

Said the cunning Spider to the Fly, "Dear friend
  what can I do,
To prove the warm affection I've always felt
  for you?
I have within my pantry, good store of all that's
  nice;
I'm sure you're very welcome—will you please
  to take a slice?"
"Oh no, no," said the little Fly, "kind Sir, that
  cannot be,
I've heard what's in your pantry, and I do not
  wish to see!"

"Sweet creature," said the Spider, "you're witty
   and you're wise;
How handsome are your gauzy wings, how
   brilliant are your eyes!
I've a little looking-glass upon my parlor shelf,
If you'll step in one moment, dear, you shall
   behold yourself."
"I thank you, gentle sir," she said, "for what
   you're pleased to say,
And bidding you good morning now, I'll call
   another day."

The Spider turned him round about, and went
   into his den,
For well he knew the silly Fly would soon come
   back again:
So he wove a subtle web, in a little corner sly,
And set his table ready, to dine upon the Fly.
Then he came out to his door again, and merrily
   did sing,

"Come hither, hither, pretty Fly, with the pearl
and silver wing;
Your robes are green and purple—there's a
crest upon your head;
Your eyes are like the diamond bright, but mine
are dull as lead!"

Alas, alas! how very soon this silly little Fly,
Hearing his wily, flattering words, came slowly
flitting by;
With buzzing wings she hung aloft, then near
and nearer drew,
Thinking only of her brilliant eyes, and green
and purple hue—
Thinking only of her crested head—poor foolish
thing! At last,
Up jumped the cunning Spider, and fiercely
held her fast.
He dragged her up his winding stair, into his
dismal den,
Within his little parlor—but she ne'er came out
again!

And now dear little children, who may this
   story read,
To idle, silly flattering words, I pray you ne'er
   give heed:
Unto an evil counsellor, close heart and ear
   and eye,
And take a lesson from this tale, of the Spider
   and the Fly.

—*Mary Howitt*

GRAND ADVENTURES

From "Auguries of Innocence"

To see a World in a grain of sand,
And a Heaven in a wild flower,
Hold Infinity in the palm of your hand,
And Eternity in an hour.

—*William Blake*

Fierce Adventures

Between the bookcase and the wall
Is raised a castle, gray and tall,
The desk top is a wooden moat,
The rocking chair's a pirate boat,—
My little boy, turned six to-day,
Has fierce adventures in his play.

My little maid goes venturing, too,
O bold grim robbers—what a crew!
She helps to take the gold—but then
She hurries back to home again
For she must set the things for tea
With beautiful house-wifery.

The table's set upon the floor,
   The pirate marches in,
And eats and eats and asks for more
With true piratic din.

O ye who never knew the life
Of dragon-hunting, golden strife
Of pirates on a windy sea
Returning meekly home for tea;
Who never heard the black knight's call?
I fear ye have not lived at all!

—*Annette Wynne*

Pirate Story

Three of us afloat in the meadow by the swing,
  Three of us aboard in the basket on the lea.
Winds are in the air, they are blowing in the
    spring,
  And waves are on the meadow like the waves
    there are at sea.

Where shall we adventure, today that we're
    afloat,
  Wary of the weather and steering by a star?
Shall it be to Africa, a-steering of the boat,
  To Providence, or Babylon, or off to Malabar?

Hi! but here's a squadron a-rowing on the sea—
  Cattle on the meadow a-charging with a roar!
Quick, and we'll escape them, they're as mad as
    they can be,
  The wicket is the harbour and the garden is
    the shore.

—*Robert Louis Stevenson*

Sea Fever

I must go down to the seas again, to the lonely
    sea and the sky,
And all I ask is a tall ship and a star to steer
    her by,
And the wheel's kick and the wind's song and
    the white sail's shaking,
And a gray mist on the sea's face, and a gray
    dawn breaking.

I must go down to the seas again, for the call of
    the running tide
Is a wild call and a clear call that may not be
    denied;
And all I ask is a windy day with the white
    clouds flying,
And the flung spray and the blown spume, and
    the sea gulls crying.

I must down to the seas again, to the vagrant
  gypsy life.
To the gull's way and the whale's way where
  the wind's like a whetted knife;
And all I ask is a merry yarn from a laughing
  fellow-rover,
And quiet sleep and a sweet dream when the
  long trick's over.

—*John Masefield*

The Cowboy's Life

The bawl of the steer,
To a cowboy's ear,
   Is music of sweetest strain;
And the yelping notes
Of the gay coyotes
   To him are a glad refrain.

For a kingly crown
In the noisy town
   His saddle he wouldn't change;
No life so free
As the life we see
   Way out on the Yaso range.

The rapid beat
Of his broncho's feet
   On the sod as he speeds along,
Keeps living time
To the ringing rhyme
   Of his rollicking cowboy song.

The winds may blow
And the thunder growl
   Or the breezes may safely moan;—
A cowboy's life
Is a royal life
   His saddle his kingly throne.

—John A. Lomax

Out Where the West Begins

Out where the handclasp's a little stronger,
Out where the smile dwells a little longer,
  That's where the West begins;
Out where the sun is a little brighter,
Where the snows that fall are a trifle whiter,
Where the bonds of home are a wee bit
    tighter,—
  That's where the West begins.

Out where the skies are a trifle bluer,
Out where friendship's a little truer,
  That's where the West begins;
Out where a fresher breeze is blowing,
Where there's laughter in every streamlet
    flowing,
Where there's more of reaping and less of
    sowing,—
  That's where the West begins.

Out where the world is in the making,
Where fewer hearts in despair are aching,
  That's where the West begins;
Where there's more of singing and less of
    sighing,
Where there's more of giving and less of buying,
And a man makes friends without half trying—
  That's where the West begins.

—*Arthur Chapman*

A Wanderer's Song

A wind's in the heart of me, a fire's in my heels,
I am tired of brick and stone and rumbling
   wagon-wheels;
I hunger for the sea's edge, the limits of the land,
Where the wild old Atlantic is shouting on the
   sand.

Oh, I'll be going, leaving the noises of the street,
To where a lifting foresail-foot is yanking at
   the sheet;
To a windy, tossing anchorage where yawls and
   ketches ride,
Oh, I'll be going, going, until I meet the tide.

And first I'll hear the sea-wind, the mewing of
   the gulls,
The clucking, sucking of the sea about the
   rusty hulls,
The songs at the capstan at the hooker warping
   out,
And then the heart of me'll know I'm there or
   thereabout.

Oh, I am sick of brick and stone, the heart of
me is sick,
For windy green, unquiet sea, the realm of
Moby Dick;
And I'll be going, going, from the roaring of
the wheels,
For a wind's in the heart of me, a fire's in my
heels.

—*John Masefield*

Travel

The railroad track is miles away,
   And the day is loud with voices speaking,
Yet there isn't a train goes by all day
   But I hear its whistle shrieking.

All night there isn't a train goes by,
   Though the night is still for sleep and
      dreaming,
But I see its cinders red on the sky,
   And hear its engine steaming.

My heart is warm with friends I make,
   And better friends I'll not be knowing;
Yet there isn't a train I'd rather take,
   No matter where it's going.

—*Edna St. Vincent Millay*

The Road Not Taken

Two roads diverged in a yellow wood,
And sorry I could not travel both
And be one traveler, long I stood
And looked down one as far as I could
To where it bent in the undergrowth;

Then took the other, as just as fair,
And having perhaps the better claim,
Because it was grassy and wanted wear;
Though as for that the passing there
Had worn them really about the same,

And both that morning equally lay
In leaves no step had trodden black.
Oh, I kept the first for another day!
Yet knowing how way leads on to way,
I doubted if I should ever come back.

I shall be telling this with a sigh
Somewhere ages and ages hence:
Two roads diverged in a wood, and I—
I took the one less traveled by,
And that has made all the difference.

—*Robert Frost*

High Flight

Oh, I have slipped the surly bonds of earth
And danced the skies on laughter-silvered
   wings;
Sunward I've climbed and joined the tumbling
   mirth
Of sun-split clouds—and done a hundred things
You have not dreamed of—wheeled and soared
   and swung
High in the sunlit silence. Hov'ring there
I've chased the shouting wind along and flung
My eager craft through footless halls of air.
Up, up the long delirious burning blue
I've topped the wind-swept heights with easy
   grace,
Where never lark, or ever eagle, flew—
And, while with silent, lifting mind I've trod
The high untrespassed sanctity of space,
Put out my hand, and touched the face of God.

—*John Gillespie Magee Jr.*

THINGS THAT GO BUMP
IN THE NIGHT

From Ghoulies and Ghosties
And long-leggity Beasties,
And all Things that go bump in the Night,
Good Lord deliver us.

Something Is There

Something is there
  there on the stair
    coming down
      coming down
        stepping with care.
          Coming down
            coming down
              slinkety-sly.

Something is coming and wants to get by.

—*Lilian Moore*

Little Orphant Annie

Little Orphant Annie's come to our house to stay,

An' wash the cups and saucers up, an' brush the
 crumbs away,

An' shoo the chickens off the porch, an' dust
 the hearth, an' sweep,

An' make the fire, an' bake the bread, an' earn
 her board-an'-keep;

An' all us other childern, when the supper-things
 is done,

We set around the kitchen fire an' has the
 mostest fun

A-list'nin' to the witch tales 'at Annie tells about,

An' the Gobble-uns 'at gits you

   Ef you

      Don't

         Watch

           Out!

Onc't they was a little boy wouldn't say his
    prayers,—
So when he went to bed at night, away upstairs,
His Mammy heerd him holler, an' his Daddy
    heerd him bawl,
An' when they turn't the kivvers down, he
    wasn't there at all!
An' they seeked him in the rafter room, an'
    cubbyhole, an' press,
An' seeked him up the chimblyflue, an'
    ever'wheres, I guess;
But all they ever found was thist his pants an'
    roundabout:—
An' the Gobble-uns 'll git you
    Ef you
        Don't
            Watch
                Out!

An' one time a little girl 'ud allus laugh an' grin,
An' make fun of ever'one, an' all her blood
   an' kin;
An' onc't, when they was "company," an' ole
   folks was there,
She mocked 'em an' shocked 'em, an' said she
   didn't care!
An' thist as she kicked her heels, an' turn't to
   run an' hide,
They was two great big Black Things a-standin'
   by her side,
An' they snatched her through the ceilin' 'fore
   she knowed what she's about!
An' the Gobble-uns 'll git you
   Ef you
      Don't
         Watch
            Out!

An' little Orphant Annie says, when the blaze
   is blue,
An' the lamp-wick sputters, an' the wind goes
   woo-oo!
An' you hear the crickets quit, an' the moon is
   gray,
An' the lightnin' bugs in dew is all squenched
   away,—
You better mind yer parents, an' yer teachers
   fond an' dear,
An' churish them 'at loves you, an' dry the
   orphant's tear,
An' he'p the pore an' needy ones 'at clusters all
   about,
Er the Gobble-uns 'll git you
   Ef you
      Don't
         Watch
            Out!

—*James Whitcomb Riley*

There was an old woman tossed up in a basket,
Ninety times as high as the moon;
Where she was going, I couldn't but ask it,
For in her hand she carried a broom.

"Old woman, old woman, old woman," quoth I,
"O whither, O whither, O whither, so high?"
"To brush the cobwebs off the sky!"
"Shall I go with thee?" "Aye, by and by."

Very Nearly

I never quite saw fairyfolk
   A-dancing in the glade,
Where, just beyond the hollow oak,
   Their broad green rings are laid;
But, while behind that oak I hid,
One day I very nearly did!

I never quite saw mermaids rise
   Above the twilight sea,
When sands, left wet, 'neath sunset skies,
   Are blushing rosily:
But—all alone, those rocks amid—
One day I very nearly did!

I never quite saw Goblin Grim,
   Who haunts our lumber room
And pops his head above the rim
   Of that oak chest's deep gloom:
But once—when mother raised the lid—
I very, very nearly did!

—*Queenie Scott-Hopper*

The Fairies

Up the airy mountain,
   Down the rushy glen,
We daren't go a-hunting
   For fear of little men;
Wee folk, good folk,
   Trooping all together;
Green jacket, red cap,
   And white owl's feather.

Down along the rocky shore
   Some make their home—
They live on crispy pancakes
   Of yellow tide-foam;
Some in the reeds
   Of the black mountain lake,
With frogs for their watch-dogs,
   All night awake.

By the craggy hill-side,
    Through the mosses bare,
They have planted thorn-trees
    For pleasure here and there.
If any man so daring
    As dig them up in spite,
He shall find their sharpest thorns
    In his bed at night.

Up the airy mountain,
    Down the rushy glen,
We daren't go a-hunting
    For fear of little men;
Wee folk, good folk,
    Trooping all together;
Green jacket, red cap,
    And white owl's feather!

—*William Allingham*

If You See a Fairy Ring

If you see a fairy ring
In a field of grass,
Very lightly step around,
Tip-toe as you pass.
Last night fairies frolicked there
And they're sleeping somewhere near.
If you see a tiny fairy
Lying fast asleep
Shut your eyes,
And run away—
Do not stay to peek!
Do not tell
Or you'll break a fairy spell.

Please Be Careful

Please be careful where you tread,
  The fairies are about;
Last night when I had gone to bed,
  I heard them creeping out.
And wouldn't it be a dreadful thing
  To do a fairy harm?
To crush a little delicate wing
  Or bruise a tiny arm?
They're all about the place, I know,
  So do be careful where you go.

—*Rose Fyleman*

In the Hours of Darkness

When the night is cloudy,
 And mists hang on the hill,
There are ghostly footsteps
 And voices, thin and shrill;
Nothing will your looking
 Show you in the dark
If the door is opened,
 But harken, harken, hark!

In the hours of darkness
 Thronging from their camp
Dark and ghostly goblins
 Flicker by the lamp;
Listen to their laughter
 As they flicker by the lamp!

When the rain is falling,
 And the night is bleak,
Something moves the knocker
 And makes the hinges creak;

Sometimes on the window
  A waving shadow falls;
Sometimes clammy whispers
  Echo through the halls.

They lure you with sweet voices
  When you should be in bed;
Something creaks behind you,
  Something creaks ahead,
Something gazes at you
  From behind a tree,
But if you look around you,
  Nothing will you see.

In the hours of darkness
  Thronging from their camp
Dark and ghostly goblins
  Flicker by the lamp;
Listen to their laughter
  As they flicker by the lamp

—*James Flexner*

LIONS AND TIGERS AND BEARS—AND MORE

The Animal Store

If I had a hundred dollars to spend,
　Or maybe a little more,
I'd hurry as fast as my legs would go
　Straight to the animal store.

I wouldn't say, "How much for this or that?"
　"What kind of dog is he?"
I'd buy as many as rolled an eye,
　Or wagged a tail at me!

I'd take the hound with the drooping ears
　That sits by himself alone;
Cockers and Cairns and wobbly pups
　For to be my very own.

I might buy a parrot all red and green,
　And the monkey I saw before,
If I had a hundred dollars to spend,
　Or maybe a little more.

—*Rachel Field*

The Tiger

Tiger! Tiger! burning bright
In the forests of the night,
What immortal hand or eye
Could frame thy fearful symmetry?

In what distant deeps or skies
Burnt the fire of thine eyes?
On what wings dare he aspire?
What the hand dare seize the fire?

And what shoulder, and what art,
Could twist the sinews of thy heart?
And when thy heart began to beat,
What dread hand? and what dread feet?

What the hammer? what the chain?
In what furnace was thy brain?
What the anvil? what dread grasp
Dare its deadly terrors clasp?

When the stars threw down their spears,
And watered heaven with their tears,
Did he smile his work to see?
Did he who made the Lamb make thee?

Tiger! Tiger! burning bright
In the forests of the night,
What immortal hand or eye
Dare frame thy fearful symmetry?

—*William Blake*

The Little Turtle

A Recitation for Martha Wakefield, Three Years Old

There was a little turtle.
He lived in a box.
He swam in a puddle.
He climbed on the rocks.

He snapped at a mosquito.
He snapped at a flea.
He snapped at a minnow.
And he snapped at me.

He caught the mosquito.
He caught the flea.
He caught the minnow.
But he didn't catch me.

—*Vachel Lindsay*

The Eagle

He clasps the crag with crooked hands;
Close to the sun in lonely lands,
Ringed with the azure world, he stands.

The wrinkled sea beneath him crawls;
He watches from his mountain walls,
And like a thunderbolt he falls.

—*Alfred, Lord Tennyson*

Four Ducks on a Pond

Four ducks on a pond,
A grass-bank beyond,
A blue sky of spring,
White clouds on the wing:
What a little thing
To remember for years—
To remember with tears!

—*William Allingham*

* * *

Swan swam over the sea,
Swim, swan, swim!
Swan swam back again,
Well swum, swan!

The Cow

The friendly cow all red and white,
   I love with all my heart:
She gives me cream with all her might,
   To eat with apple tart.

She wanders lowing here and there,
   And yet she cannot stray,
All in the pleasant open air,
   The pleasant light of day;

And blown by all the winds that pass
   And wet with all the showers,
She walks among the meadow grass
   And eats the meadow flowers.

—*Robert Louis Stevenson*

Mary Had a Little Lamb

Mary had a little lamb,
    Its fleece was white as snow;
And everywhere that Mary went,
    The lamb was sure to go.

He followed her to school one day—
    That was against the rule.
It made the children laugh and play
    To see a lamb at school.

So the teacher turned him out,
    But still he lingered near,
And waited patiently about,
    Till Mary did appear.

Then he ran to her, and laid
    His head upon her arm,
As if he said, "I'm not afraid—
    You'll shield me from all harm."

"Why makes the lamb love Mary so?"
  The little children cry.
"Oh, Mary loves the lamb, you know,"
  The teacher did reply,

"And you each gentle animal
  In confidence may bind
And make it follow at your call,
  If you are always kind."

—*Sarah Josepha Hale*

The Cat of Cats

I am the cat of cats. I am
   The everlasting cat!
Cunning, and old, and sleek as jam,
   The everlasting cat!
I hunt vermin in the night—
   The everlasting cat!
For I see best without the light—
   The everlasting cat!

—*William Brighty Rands*

The Three Little Kittens

Three little kittens lost their mittens;
   And they began to cry,
      "Oh, mother dear,
      We very much fear
That we have lost our mittens."
      "Lost your mittens!
      You naughty kittens!
Then you shall have no pie!"
         "Mee-ow, mee-ow, mee-ow."
"No, you shall have no pie."
         "Mee-ow, mee-ow, mee-ow."

The three little kittens found their mittens,
   And they began to cry,
      "Oh, mother dear,
      See here, see here!
See, we have found our mittens."
      "Put on your mittens,
      You silly kittens,

And you may have some pie."
    "Purr-r, purr-r, purr-r,
Oh, let us have the pie!
    Purr-r, purr-r, purr r."

The three little kittens put on their mittens,
  And soon ate up the pie;
    "Oh, mother dear,
    We greatly fear
That we have soiled our mittens."
    "Soiled your mittens!
    You naughty kittens!"
Then they began to sigh,
    "Mee-ow, mee-ow, mee-ow."
Then they began to sigh,
    "Mee-ow, mee-ow, mee-ow."

The three little kittens washed their mittens,
  And hung them out to dry;
    "Oh, mother dear,
    Do not you hear,

That we have washed our mittens?"
  "Washed your mittens?
  O, you're good kittens.
But I smell a rat close by,
    Hush! hush! mee-ow, mee-ow."
"We smell a rat close by,
    Mee-ow, mee-ow, mee-ow."

—*Eliza Lee Follen*

Lone Dog

I'm a lean dog, a keen dog, a wild dog, and lone;
I'm a rough dog, a tough dog, hunting on my
   own;
I'm a bad dog, a mad dog, teasing silly sheep;
I love to sit and bay the moon, to keep fat souls
   from sleep.

I'll never be a lap dog, licking dirty feet,
A sleek dog, a meek dog, cringing for my meat,
Not for me the fireside, the well-filled plate,
But shut door, and sharp stone, and cuff and
   kick and hate.

Not for me the other dogs, running by my side,
Some have run a short while, but none of them
   would bide,
Oh, mine is still the lone trail, the hard trail,
   the best,
Wide wind, and wild stars, and hunger of the
   quest!

—*Irene McLeod*

OUR GREAT, WIDE, BEAUTIFUL, WONDERFUL WORLD

The World

Great, wide, beautiful, wonderful World,
With the wonderful water round you curled,
And the wonderful grass upon your breast—
World, you are beautifully drest.

The wonderful air is over me,
And the wonderful wind is shaking the tree,
It walks on the water, and whirls the mills,
And talks to itself on the tops of the hills.

You friendly Earth! how far do you go,
With the wheatfields that nod and the rivers
    that flow,
With cities and gardens, and cliffs, and isles,
And people upon you for thousands of miles?

Ah, you are so great, and I am so small,
I tremble to think of you, World, at all;
And yet, when I said my prayers today,
A whisper inside me seemed to say,
"You are more than the Earth, though you are
    such a dot:
You can love and think, and the Earth cannot."

—*William Brighty Rands*

I'm Glad the Sky
Is Painted Blue

I'm glad the sky is painted blue,
   And the earth is painted green,
With such a lot of nice fresh air
   All sandwiched in between.

Out in the Fields with God

The little cares that fretted me,
  I lost them yesterday,
Among the fields above the sea,
  Among the winds at play,
Among the lowing of the herds,
  The rustling of the trees,
Among the singing of the birds,
  The humming of the bees.
The foolish fears of what might pass
  I cast them all away
Among the clover-scented grass
  Among the new-mown hay,
Among the hushing of the corn
  Where drowsy poppies nod,
Where ill thoughts die and good are born—
  Out in the fields with God.

All Things Bright and Beautiful

All things bright and beautiful,
  All creatures great and small,
All things wise and wonderful,
  The Lord God made them all.

Each little flower that opens,
  Each little bird that sings,
He made their glowing colors,
  He made their tiny wings.

The purple-headed mountain,
  The river running by,
The sunset, and the morning,
  That brightens up the sky;

The cold wind in the winter,
  The pleasant summer sun,
The ripe fruits in the garden,
  He made them every one.

The tall trees in the greenwood,
  The meadows where we play,
The rushes by the water
  We gather every day—

He gave us eyes to see them,
  And lips that we might tell,
How great is God Almighty,
  Who has made all things well.

—*Cecil Frances Alexander*

Pied Beauty

Glory be to God for dappled things—
   For skies of couple-color as a brinded cow;
     For rose-moles all in stipple upon trout
      that swim;
Fresh-firecoal chestnut-falls; finches' wings;
   Landscape plotted and pieced—fold, fallow,
     and plough;
     And all trades, their gear and tackle and
      trim.

All things counter, original, spare, strange;
   Whatever is fickle, freckled (who knows how?)
     With swift, slow; sweet, sour; adazzle, dim;
He fathers-forth whose beauty is past change:
     Praise Him.

—*Gerard Manley Hopkins*

Color

What is pink? A rose is pink
By the fountain's brink.
What is red? A poppy's red
In its barley bed.
What is blue? The sky's blue
Where the clouds float through.
What is white? A swan is white
Sailing in the light.
What is yellow? Pears are yellow,
Rich, ripe and mellow.
What is green? The grass is green,
With small flowers between.
What is violet? Clouds are violet
In the summer twilight.
What is orange? Why, an orange,
Just an orange!

—*Christina Rossetti*

Flint

An emerald is as green as grass,
A ruby red as blood;
A sapphire shines as blue as heaven;
A flint lies in the mud.

A diamond is a brilliant stone,
To catch the world's desire;
An opal holds a brilliant spark;
But a flint holds fire.

—*Christina Rossetti*

Red Geraniums

Life did not bring me silken gowns,
Nor jewels for my hair,
Nor signs of gabled foreign towns
In distant countries fair,
But I can glimpse, beyond my pane, a green
    and friendly hill,
And red geraniums aflame upon my window sill.

The brambled cares of everyday,
The tiny humdrum things,
May bind my feet when they would stray,
But still my heart has wings
While red geraniums are bloomed against my
    window glass,
And low above my green-sweet hill the gypsy
    wind-clouds pass.

And if my dreamings ne'er come true,
The brightest and the best,
But leave me lone my journey through,
I'll set my heart at rest,
And thank God for home-sweet things, a green
and friendly hill,
And red geraniums aflame upon my window sill.

—*Martha Haskell Clark*

Daffodils

I wandered lonely as a cloud
   That floats on high o'er vales and hills,
When all at once I saw a crowd,—
   A host of golden daffodils
Beside the lake, beneath the trees,
Fluttering and dancing in the breeze.

Continuous as the stars that shine
   And twinkle on the Milky Way,
They stretched in never-ending line
   Along the margin of a bay:
Ten thousand saw I, at a glance,
Tossing their heads in sprightly dance.

The waves beside them danced, but they
   Outdid the sparkling waves in glee;
A poet could not but be gay
   In such a jocund company;
I gazed—and gazed—but little thought
What wealth the show to me had brought.

For oft, when on my couch I lie,
    In vacant or in pensive mood,
They flash upon that inward eye
    Which is the bliss of solitude;
And then my heart with pleasure fills,
And dances with the daffodils.

—*William Wordsworth*

Trees

I think that I shall never see
A poem lovely as a tree.

A tree whose hungry mouth is pressed
Against the earth's sweet flowing breast;

A tree that looks at God all day
And lifts her leafy arms to pray;

A tree that may in summer wear
A nest of robins in her hair;

Upon whose bosom snow has lain;
Who intimately lives with rain.

Poems are made by fools like me,
But only God can make a tree.

—*Joyce Kilmer*

The Sea! The Sea!

The sea! The sea! The open sea!
The blue, the fresh, the ever free!
Without a mark, without a bound,
It runneth the earth's wide region round,
It play with the clouds; it mocks the skies,
Or like a cradled creature lies.

—*Barry Cornwall*

The Sea Shell

Sea Shell, Sea Shell,
Sing me a song, O please!
A song of ships and sailor-men
Of parrots and tropical trees;
Of islands lost in the Spanish Main
Which no man may find again,
Of fishes and corals under the waves,
And sea-horses stabled in great green caves

Sea Shell, Sea Shell,
Sing me a song, O please.

—*Amy Lowell*

Until I Saw the Sea

Until I saw the sea
I did not know
that wind
could wrinkle water so.

I never knew
that sun
could splinter a whole sea of blue.

Nor
did I know before,
a sea breathes in and out
upon a shore.

—*Lilian Moore*

WIND AND RAIN AND SNOW

Whether the Weather Be Fine

Whether the weather be fine
Or whether the weather be not
Whether the weather be cold
Or whether the weather be hot—
We'll weather the weather
Whatever the weather
Whether we like it or not!

Rain, rain, go away.
Come again another day.
Little Johnny wants to play.

* * *

When the wind is in the East,
'Tis neither good for man nor beast;
When the wind is in the North,
The skillful fisher goes not forth;
When the wind is in the South,
It blows the bait in the fishes' mouth;
When the wind is in the West,
Then 'tis at the very best.

If woolly fleeces spread the heavenly way,
No rain, be sure, disturbs the summer's day.
When clouds appear like rocks and towers,
The earth's refreshed by frequent showers.

*   *   *

Red sky at night,
Sailors delight.
Red sky at morning,
Sailors take warning.

Clouds

White sheep, white sheep,
On a blue hill,
When the wind stops
You all stand still.
When the wind blows
You walk away slow.
White sheep, white sheep,
Where do you go?

—*Christina Rossetti*

Fog

The fog comes
on little cat feet.

It sits looking
over harbor and city
on silent haunches
and then moves on.

—Carl Sandburg

I Like It When It's Mizzly

I like it when it's mizzly
and just a little drizzly
so everything looks far away
and make-believe and frizzly.

I like it when it's foggy
and sounding very froggy.
I even like it when it rains
on streets and weepy windowpanes
and catkins in the poplar tree
and *me.*

Aileen Fisher

Windy Nights

Whenever the moon and stars are set,
  Whenever the wind is high,
All night long in the dark and wet,
A man goes riding by.
Late in the night when the fires are out,
Why does he gallop and gallop about?

Whenever the trees are crying aloud,
  And ships are tossed at sea,
By, on the highway, low and loud,
  By at the gallop goes he;
By at the gallop he goes, and then
By he comes back at the gallop again.

—*Robert Louis Stevenson*

Who Has Seen the Wind?

Who has seen the wind?
Neither I nor you:
But when the leaves hang trembling,
The wind is passing through.

Who has seen the wind?
Neither you nor I.
But when the trees bow down their heads,
The wind is passing by.

—*Christina Rossetti*

The Wind

I saw you toss the kites on high
And blow the birds about the sky;
And all around I heard you pass,
Like ladies' skirts across the grass—
   O wind, a-blowing all day long,
   O wind, that sings so loud a song!

I saw the different things you did,
But always you yourself you hid.
I felt you push, I heard you call,
I could not see yourself at all—
   O wind, a-blowing all day long,
   O wind, that sings so loud a song!

O you that are so strong and cold,
O blower, are you young or old?
Are you a beast of field and tree,
Or just a stronger child than me?
   O wind, a-blowing all day long,
   O wind, that sings so loud a song!

—*Robert Louis Stevenson*

Rain in Summer

How beautiful is the rain!
After the dust and heat,
In the broad and fiery street,
In the narrow lane,
How beautiful is the rain!

How it clatters along the roofs,
Like the tramp of hoofs!
How it gushes and struggles out
From the throat of the overflowing spout!

Across the window-pane
It pours and pours;
And swift and wide,
With a muddy tide,
Like a river down the gutter roars
The rain, the welcome rain!

—*Henry Wadsworth Longfellow*

Rain

The rain is raining all around,
It falls on field and tree,
It rains on the umbrellas here,
And on the ships at sea.

—*Robert Louis Stevenson*

*   *   *

The lightning and thunder
They go and come;
But the stars and the stillness
Are always at home.

—*George Macdonald*

The Storm

See lightning is flashing,
The forest is crashing,
The rain will come dashing,
   A flood will be rising anon;

The heavens are scowling,
The thunder is growling,
The loud winds are howling,
   The storm has come suddenly on!

But now the sky clears,
The bright sun appears,
Now nobody fears,
   But soon every cloud will be gone.

—*Sara Coleridge*

The Rainbow

My heart leaps up when I behold
    A rainbow in the sky:
So was it when my life began;
So is it now I am a man;
So be it when I shall grow old,
    Or let me die!
The Child is father of the Man;
And I could wish my days to be
Bound each to each by natural piety.

—*William Wordsworth*

Velvet Shoes

Let us walk in the white snow
   In a soundless space;
With footsteps quiet and slow,
   At a tranquil pace,
   Under veils of white lace.

I shall go shod in silk,
   And you in wool,
White as a white cow's milk,
   More beautiful
   Than the breast of a gull.

We shall walk through the still town
   In a windless peace,
We shall step upon white down,
   Upon silver fleece,
   Upon softer than these.

We shall walk in velvet shoes:
    Wherever we go
Silence will fall like dews
    On white silence below.
    We shall walk in the snow.

—*Elinor Wylie*

SUN AND MOON
AND STARS

The Sun

Long before the postman comes
   The sun begins to rise,
Far in the East if you should look
   You'd find it in the skies.
At first it's just a streak of light
Then all at once the world gets bright.

Then in the sky from East to West
   The happy sun goes on its way,
And all day long it shines its best
   To give us pleasant day.
Dear God, who made the day and night,
We thank Thee for the sun's good light.

—*Annette Wynne*

Merry Sunshine

"Good morning, Merry Sunshine,
　　How did you wake so soon?
You've scared the little stars away,
　　And shined away the moon.
I watched you go to sleep last night
　　Before I stopped my playing;
How did you get way over there?
　　And where have you been staying?"

"I never go to sleep, dear child,
　　I just go round to see
My little children of the East,
　　Who rise to watch for me.
I waken all the birds and bees
　　And flowers on my way,
Then now come back to see the child
　　Who stayed out late to play."

Pippa's Song

The year's at the spring,
And day's at the morn;
Morning's at seven;
The hill-side's dew-pearl'd;
The lark's on the wing;
The snail's on the thorn;
God's in His heaven—
All's right with the world!

—*Robert Browning*

One Misty, Moisty, Morning

One misty, moisty, morning,
    When cloudy was the weather,
I chanced to meet an old man,
    Clothed all in leather.
He began to compliment
    And I began to grin.
How do you do? And how do you do?
    And how do you do again?

Bed in Summer

In winter I get up at night
And dress by yellow candle-light.
In summer, quite the other way,
I have to go to bed by day.

I have to go to bed and see
The birds still hopping on the tree,
Or hear the grown-up people's feet
Still going past me in the street.

And does it not seem hard to you,
When all the sky is clear and blue,
And I should like so much to play,
To have to go to bed by day?

—*Robert Louis Stevenson*

Night

Stars over snow,
    And in the west a planet
Swinging below a star—
    Look for a lovely thing and you will find it,
It is not far—
    It never will be far.

—*Sara Teasdale*

Lady Moon

Lady Moon, Lady Moon, where are you roving?
  Over the sea.
Lady Moon, Lady Moon, whom are you loving?
  All that love me.

Are you not tired with rolling and never
  Resting to sleep?
Why look so pale, and so sad, as for ever
  Wishing to weep?

Ask me not this, little child, if you love me;
  You are too bold;
I must obey my dear Father above me,
  And do as I'm told.

Lady Moon, Lady Moon, where are you roving?
  Over the sea.
Lady Moon, Lady Moon, whom are you loving?
  All that love me.

—*Richard Monckton Milnes*

Mockery

Happened that the moon was up before I went
  to bed,
Poking through the bramble trees her round
  gold head.
I didn't stop for stocking,
I didn't stop for shoe,
But went running out to meet her—oh, the
  night was blue!

Barefoot down the hill road, dust beneath my
  toes;
Barefoot in the pasture smelling sweet of fern
  and rose!
Oh, night was running with me,
Tame folk were all in bed—
And the moon was just showing her wild gold
  head.

But before I reached the hilltop where the
    bramble trees are tall,
I looked to see my lady moon—she wasn't
    there at all!—
Not sitting on the hilltop,
Nor slipping through the air,
Nor hanging in the brambles by her bright
    gold hair!

I walked slowly down the pasture and slowly
    up the hill,
Wondering and wondering, and very, very still.
I wouldn't look behind me,
I went at once to bed—
And poking through the window was her bold
    gold head!

—*Katherine Dixon Riggs*

Moon, So Round and Yellow

Moon, so round and yellow,
Looking from on high,
How I love to see you
Shining in the sky.
Oft and oft I wonder,
When I see you there,
How they get to light you,
Hanging in the air.

When you go at morning,
When the night is past,
And the sun comes peeping
O'er the hills at last.
Sometime I will watch you
Slyly overhead,
When you think I'm sleeping
Snugly in my bed.

—*Matthias Barr*

The Moon

The moon has a face like the clock in the hall;
She shines on thieves on the garden wall,
On streets and fields and harbour quays,
And birdies asleep in the forks of the trees.

The squalling cat and the squeaking mouse,
The howling dog by the door of the house,
The bat that lies in bed at noon,
All love to be out by the light of the moon.

But all of the things that belong to the day
Cuddle to sleep to be out of her way;
And flowers and children close their eyes
Till up in the morning the sun shall arise.

—*Robert Louis Stevenson*

I see the moon,
And the moon sees me.
God bless the moon,
And God bless me.

* * *

Star light, star bright,
Very first star I've seen tonight;
I wish you may, I wish you might
Give me the wish I wish tonight.

Stars

The stars are too many to count.
The stars make sixes and sevens.
The stars tell nothing—and everything.
The stars look scattered.
Stars are so far away they never speak when
  spoken to.

—*Carl Sandburg*

Stars

Alone in the night on a dark hill
With pines around me—Spicy and still
And a heaven full of stars, over my head,
White and topaz, and misty red;

Myriads with beating hearts of fire
That aeons, cannot vex or tire;
Up the dome of heaven, like a great hill,
I watch them marching, stately and still

And yes, I know that I, am honored to be,
Witness, of so much majesty.

—*Sara Teasdale*

The Star

Twinkle, twinkle, little star,
How I wonder what you are!
Up above the world so high,
Like a diamond in the sky.

When the blazing sun is gone,
When he nothing shines upon,
Then you show your little light,
Twinkle, twinkle, all the night.

Then the traveler in the dark,
Thanks you for your tiny spark,
He could not see which way to go,
If you did not twinkle so.

In the dark blue sky you keep,
And often through my curtains peep,
For you never shut your eye,
Till the sun is in the sky.

As your bright and tiny spark,
Lights the traveler in the dark—
Though I know not what you are,
Twinkle, twinkle, little star.

—*Jane Taylor*

BEDTIME BLESSINGS

Tumbling

In jumping and tumbling
  We spend the whole day,
Till night by arriving
  Has finished our play.

What then? One and all,
  There's no more to be said,
As we tumbled all day,
  So we tumble to bed.

Nurse's Song

When the voices of children are heard on the
    green
  And laughing is heard on the hill,
My heart is at rest within my breast,
  And everything else is still.

"Then come home, my children, the sun is gone
    down.
  And the dews of night arise;
Come, come, leave off play, and let us away
  Till the morning appears in the skies."

"No, no, let us play, for it is yet day,
  And we cannot go to sleep;
Besides in the sky the little birds fly,
  And the hills are all covered with sheep."

"Well, well, go and play till the light fades away,
And then go home to bed."
The little ones leaped and shouted and laughed;
And all the hills echoed.

—*William Blake* ·

The Sugarplum Tree

Have you ever heard of the Sugarplum Tree?
  'Tis a marvel of great renown!
It blooms on the shore of the Lollypop Sea
  In the garden of Shut-Eye Town;
The fruit that it bears is so wondrously sweet
  (As those who have tasted it say)
That good little children have only to eat
  Of that fruit to be happy next day.

When you've got to the tree, you would have a
    hard time
  To capture the fruit which I sing;
The tree is so tall that no person could climb
  To the boughs where the sugarplums swing!
But up in that tree sits a chocolate cat,
  And a gingerbread dog prowls below—
And this is the way you contrive to get at
Those sugarplums tempting you so:

You say but the word to that gingerbread dog
   And he barks with such a terrible zest
That the chocolate cat is at once all agog,
   As her swelling proportions attest.
And the chocolate cat goes cavorting around
   From this leafy limb unto that,
And the sugarplums tumble, of course, to the
     ground—
   Hurray for that chocolate cat!

There are marshmallows, gumdrops, and
     peppermint canes,
   With striping of scarlet and gold,
And you carry away of the treasure that rains,
   As much as your apron can hold!
So come, little child, cuddle closer to me
   In your dainty white nightcap and gown,
And I'll rock you away to the Sugarplum Tree
   In the garden of Shut-Eye Town.

—*Eugene Field*

Wynken, Blynken, and Nod

Wynken, Blynken, and Nod one night
   Sailed off in a wooden shoe,—
Sailed on a river of misty light
   Into a sea of dew.
"Where are you going, and what do you wish?"
   The old moon asked the three.
"We have come to fish for the herring-fish
   That live in this beautiful sea;
   Nets of silver and gold have we!"
      Said Wynken,
      Blynken,
      And Nod.

The old moon laughed and sang a song,
   As they rocked in the wooden shoe,
And the wind that sped them all night long
   Ruffled the waves of dew.
The little stars were the herring fish
   That lived in the beautiful sea—

"Now cast your nets wherever you wish,—
    Never afeard are we!"
  So cried the stars to the fishermen three,
        Wynken,
        Blynken,
        And Nod.

All night long their nets they threw
  To the stars in the twinkling foam,—
Then down from the skies came the wooden
      shoe,
  Bringing the fishermen home:
'Twas all so pretty a sail, it seemed
  As if it could not be;
And some folks thought 'twas a dream they'd
      dreamed
  Of sailing that beautiful sea;
  But I shall name you the fishermen three:
        Wynken,
        Blynken,
        And Nod.

Wynken and Blynken are two little eyes,
   And Nod is a little head,
And the wooden shoe that sailed the skies
   Is a wee one's trundle-bed;
So shut your eyes while Mother sings
   Of the wonderful sights that be,
And you shall see the beautiful things
   As you rock in the misty sea
   Where the old shoe rocked the fishermen
      three:—
         Wynken,
         Blynken,
         And Nod.

—*Eugene Field*

A Child's Thought of God

They say that God lives very high!
  But if you look above the pines
You cannot see our God. And why?

And if you dig down in the mines
  You never see Him in the gold,
Though from Him all that's glory shines.

God is so good, He wears a fold
  Of heaven and earth across His face—
Like secrets kept, for love, untold.

But still I feel that His embrace
  Slides down by thrills, through all things made,
Through sight and sound of every place:

As if my tender mother laid
  On my shut lids her kisses' pressure,
Half-waking me at night; and said,
    "Who kissed you through the dark, dear
      guesser?"

—*Elizabeth Barrett Browning*

A Little Hymn

God is so good that He will hear,
　　Whenever children humbly pray;
He always lends a gracious ear
　　To what the youngest child can say.

—*Jane Taylor*

* * *

God Watches Us

God watches o'er us all the day,
　　at home, at school, and at our play;
And when the sun has left the skies,
　　he watches with a million eyes.

—*Gabriel Setoun*

Can a Little Child Like Me

Can a little child like me
Thank the Father fittingly?
Yes, oh yes! be good and true,
Faithful, kind, in all you do;
Love the Lord, and do your part;
Learn to say with all your heart,

Father, we thank Thee,
Father, we thank Thee,
Father, in Heaven, we thank Thee!

—*Mary Mapes Dodge*

God be in my head, and in my understanding;
God be in my eyes, and in my looking;
God be in my mouth, and in my speaking;
God be in my heart, and in my thinking;
God be at my end and at my departing.

—*The Sarum Missal*

* * *

I Thank You, God

I thank you, God,
For a hundred things:
For the flower that blooms,
For the bird that sings,
For the sun that shines,
And the rain that drops,
For ice cream,
    and raisins,
      and lollipops.
        Amen.

Goodnight! Goodnight!
  Far flies the light;
  But still God's love
  Shall flame above,
  Making all bright.
Goodnight! Goodnight!

—*Victor Hugo*

*   *   *

Happy Thought

The world is so full of a number of things,
  I'm sure we should all be as happy as kings.

—*Robert Louis Stevenson*

A Child's Prayer [Or, Hymn]

God, make my life a little light
   Within the world to glow;
A little flame that burneth bright,
   Wherever I may go.

God, make my life a little flower
   That giveth joy to all,
Content to bloom in native bower,
   Although the place be small.

God, make my life a little song
   That comforteth the sad;
That helpeth others to be strong,
   And makes the singer glad.

God, make my life a little staff
   Whereon the weak may rest,
That so what health and strength I have
   May serve my neighbors best.

God, make my life a little hymn
　　Of tenderness and praise;
Of faith that never waxeth dim.
　　In all His wondrous ways.

—*Matilda Barbara Betham-Edwards*

Cradle Song

Ere the moon begins to rise
  Or a star to shine,
All the bluebells close their eyes—
  So close thine,
    Thine, dear, thine!

Birds are sleeping in the nest
  On the swaying bough,
Thus, against the mother's breast—
  So sleep thou—
    Sleep, sleep, thou!

—*Thomas Bailey Aldrich*

A Cradle Song

The angels are stooping
Above your bed;
They weary of trooping
With the whimpering dead.

God's laughing in Heaven
To see you so good;
The Sailing Seven
Are gay with His mood.

I sigh that kiss you,
For I must own
That I shall miss you
When you have grown.

—*W. B. Yeats*

Hush, little baby, don't say a word.
Papa's gonna buy you a mockingbird.
And if that mockingbird won't sing,
Papa's gonna buy you a diamond ring.

And if that diamond ring is brass,
Papa's gonna buy you a looking glass.
And if that looking glass gets broke,
Papa's gonna buy you a billy goat.

And if that billy goat won't pull,
Papa's gonna buy you a cart and bull.
And if that cart and bull turn over,
Papa's gonna buy you a dog named Rover.

And if that dog named Rover won't bark,
Papa's gonna buy you a horse and cart.
And if that horse and cart fall down,
You'll still be the sweetest little baby in town.

Lullaby

Lullaby, oh, lullaby!
Flowers are closed and lambs are sleeping;
Lullaby, oh, lullaby!
Stars are up, the moon is peeping;
Lullaby, oh, lullaby!
While the birds are silence keeping,
Lullaby, oh, lullaby!
Sleep, my baby, fall a-sleeping,
Lullaby, oh, lullaby!

—*Christina Rossetti*

*   *   *

Rock-a-bye baby, in the treetop
When the wind blows, the cradle will rock
When the bough breaks, the cradle will fall
And down will come baby, cradle and all

In the Tree-Top

"Rock-a-by, baby, up in the tree-top!"
  Mother his blanket is spinning;
And a light little rustle that never will stop,
  Breezes and boughs are beginning.
Rock-a-by, baby, swinging so high!
    Rock-a-by!

"When the wind blows, then the cradle will
    rock."
  Hush! now it stirs in the bushes;
Now with a whisper, a flutter of talk,
  Baby and hammock it pushes.
Rock-a-by, baby! Shut, pretty eye!
    Rock-a-by!

"Rock with the boughs, rock-a-by, baby, dear!"
  Leaf-tongues are singing and saying;
Mother she listens, and sister is near,
  Under the tree softly playing.
Rock-a-by, baby! Mother's close by!
    Rock-a-by!

Weave him a beautiful dream, little breeze!
   Little leaves, nestle around him!
He will remember the song of the trees,
   When age with silver has crowned him.
Rock-a-by, baby! Wake by and by!
      Rock-a-by!

—*Lucy Larcom*

PERMISSIONS ACKNOWLEDGMENTS ∽

Reiner on behalf of the Boulder Public Library Foundation, Inc.

JAMES FLEXNER
"In the Hours of Darkness" from *Creative Youth* by Hyghes Mearns, copyright © 1925 by Doubleday, a division of Random House, Inc.

ROSE FYLEMAN
"Please Be Careful" by Rose Fyleman. Used by permission of The Society of Authors as the Literary Representatives of the Estate of Rose Fyleman.

ARTHUR GUITERMAN
"Routine" by Arthur Guiterman, reprinted with the permission of Richard Sclove.

LANGSTON HUGHES
"Hold Fast To Dreams" by Langston Hughes. From The Collected Poems of Langston Hughes by Langston Hughes, copyright © 1994 by the Estate of Langston Hughes. Used by permission of Alfred A. Knopf, a division of Random House. Reprinted by permission of Harold Ober Associates Incorporated.

RUDYARD KIPLING
"If" by Rudyard Kipling is used by permission of A. B. Watt Ltd on behalf of The National Trust for Places of Historic Interest or Natural Beauty.

INDEX OF AUTHORS

A
Aldis, Dorothy, 35
Aldrich, Thomas Bailey, 223
Alexander, Cecil Frances, 160
Allingham, William, 38, 132, 145
Anthony, Edward, 60
Author unknown, 4, 11, 22, 26, 27, 28, 49, 51, 52, 53, 60, 73, 74, 75, 76, 77, 89, 124, 130, 134, 145, 158, 159, 174, 175, 176, 191, 193, 201, 208, 219, 225, 226

B
Barr, Matthias, 199
Beeching, Henry Charles, 33
Betham-Edwards, Matilda Barbara, 221
Bishop, Morris, 79
Blake, William, 106, 141, 209
Boyden, Polly Chase, 37, 42
Bracket, Joseph, Jr., 64
Browning, Elizabeth Barrett, 216
Browning, Robert, 192
Burgess, Frank Gelett, 77
Burgess, Gelett, 54
Burns, Robert, 50

C
Carney, Julia Fletcher, 62
Carroll, Lewis, 47, 70, 80
Chapman, Arthur, 114
Chute, Marchette, 10
Clark, Martha Haskell, 165
Coleridge, Sara, 185
Cornwall, Barry, 170

D
de la Mare, Walter, 5, 46
Dickinson, Emily, 9, 61, 65, 86
Dodge, Mary Mapes, 218

F
Farjeon, Eleanor, v
Field, Eugene, 92, 211, 213
Field, Rachel, 140
Fisher, Aileen, 179
Flexner, James, 136
Follen, Eliza Lee, 150
Frost, Robert, 23, 119
Fyleman, Rose, 135

G
Goodrich, Samuel Griswold, 78
Greenaway, Kate, 25
Guiterman, Arthur, Guiterman, Arthur

H
Hale, Sarah Josepha, 147
Hogg, James, 31
Hopkins, Gerard Manley, 162
Howitt, Mary, 99
Hughes, Langston, 68
Hugo, Victor, 220

K
Kilmer, Joyce, 169
Kingsley, Charles, 41
Kipling, Rudyard, 66

L
Larcom, Lucy, 227
Lear, Edward, 73, 94
LeGallienne, Richard, 29
Lindsay, Vachel, 143
Lomax, John A., 112
Longfellow, Henry Wadsworth, 183
Lowell, Amy, 171

M

Macdonald, George, 184
Magee, John Gillespie, Jr., 121
Mansfield, Katherine, 17
Markham, Edwin, 58
Masefield, John, 110, 116
McLeod, Irene, 153
Merriam, Eve, 13
Millay, Edna St.Vincent, 2, 118
Milligan, Spike, 83
Milne, A. A., 59
Milnes, Richard Monckton, 196
Moore, Lilian, 125, 172
Morley, Christopher Darlington, 44

N

Noyes, Alfred, 15

R

Rands, William Brighty, 149, 156
Richards, Laura Elizabeth, 72
Riggs, Katherine Dixon, 197
Riley, James Whitcomb, 126
Ross, A. B., 16
Rossetti, Christina, 163, 164, 177, 181, 226
Russell, George William ("Æ"), 24

S

Sandburg, Carl, 178, 202
Sarum Missal, The, 219

Saxe

Saxe, John Godfrey, 96
Scott-Hopper, Queenie, 131
Setoun, Gabriel, 217
Smith, Stevie, 14
Speyer, Leonora, 3
Stevenson, Robert Louis, 7, 30, 40, 55, 87, 90, 109, 146, 180, 182, 184, 194, 200, 220

T

Taggard, Genevieve, 48
Taylor, Jane, 204, 217
Teasdale, Sara, 63, 195, 203
Tennyson, Alfred, Lord, 144

V

Van Rensselaer, Mariana Griswold, 19

W

Watts, Isaac, 18
Wesley, John, 50
Wordsworth, William, 167, 186
Wylie, Elinor, 187
Wynne, Annette, 107, 190

Y

Yeats, W. B., 224

INDEX OF TITLES 〜

A
Afternoon on a Hill, 2
All Things Bright and Beautiful, 160
Animal Crackers, 44
Animal Store, The, 140
"Auguries of Innocence," From, 106

B
Bad Report—Good Manners, 83
Barter, 63
Bed in Summer, 194
Bicycling Song, 33
Blind Men and the Elephant, The, 96
Book, A, 86
Boy's Song, A, 31

C
Can a Little Child Like Me, 218
Cat of Cats, The, 149
Chartless, 61
Child's Prayer [Or Hymn], A, 221
Child's Thought of God, A, 216
Clouds, 177
Color, 169
Come Out to Play, 99
Cow, The, 146
Cowboy's Life, The, 112
Cradle Song, 223
Cradle Song, A, 224
Crust of Bread, The, 49
Cupboard, The, 46

D
Daddy Fell into the Pond, 15
Daffodils, 167
Duel, The, 92

E
Eagle, The, 144
Eletelephony, 72

F
Fairies, The, 132
Fierce Adventures, 107
Flint, 164
Fog, 178
Four Ducks on a Pond, 145
Frolic, 24

G
Gardener's Song, The, 80
God Watches Us, 217
Good Play, A, 30
Goops, The, 54

H
Happy Thought, 220
Hiding, 35
Higglety, Pigglety, Pop!, 78
High Flight, 121
Hold Fast to Dreams, 68
Human Affection, 14

I
I Like It When It's Mizzly, 179
I Meant to Do My Work Today, 29
I Thank You, God, 219
If, 66
If I Can Stop One Heart From Breaking, 65
If You See a Fairy Ring, 134
I'm Glad the Sky Is Painted Blue, 158
"I'm nobody! Who are you?," 9
In the Hours of Darkness, 136
In the Tree-Top, 227

J

Jabberwocky, 70

L

Lady Moon, 196
Land of Story-Books, The, 90
Little Brother's Secret, 17
Little Hymn, A, 217
Little Orphant Annie, 126
Little Things, 62
Little Turtle, The, 143
Lone Dog, 153
Love Between Brothers and
  Sisters, 18
Lullaby, 226

M

Manners, 19
Mary Had a Little Lamb, 147
Me, 5
Measure Me, Sky!, 3
Merry Sunshine, 191
Millions of Strawberries, 48
Mockery, 197
Moon, So Round and Yellow, 199
Moon, The, 200
Mr. Nobody, 11
Mud!, 37
My Little Doll, from *The Water-
  Babies*, 41
My Shadow, 7
Myself, 4

N

Night, 195
Nurse's Song, 209

O

One Misty, Moisty, Morning,
  193
Out in the Fields with God,
  159
Out Where the West Begins,
  114
Owl and the Pussy Cat, The,
  94

P

Pasture, The, 23
Pied Beauty, 162
Pippa's Song, 192
Pirate Story, 109
Please Be Careful, 135
Poetry, v
Politeness, 59
Purple Cow, The, 77

R

Rain, 184
Rain in Summer, 183
Rainbow, The, 186
Red Geraniums, 165
Ring-a-Ring, 25
Road Not Taken, The, 119
Routine, 84
Rules for the Road, 58

S

Sea Fever, 110
Sea Shell, The, 171
Sea! The Sea!, The, 170
Self-Control, 42
Simple Gifts, 64
Something Is There, 125
Song of Sixpence, A, 26
Song of the Pop-Bottlers,
  79
Spider and the Fly, The, 99
Star, The, 204
Stars, 202, 203
Storm, The, 185
Sugarplum Tree, The, 211
Sun, The, 190
Swing, The, 40
Swing Song, A, 38

T

Table Graces, 50
Three Little Kittens, The,
  150
Tiger, The, 141
To Any Reader, 87
Travel, 118

Trees, 169
Tumbling, 208
Turtle Soup, 47
Two in Bed, 16
Two People, 13

U
Until I Saw the Sea, 172

V
Velvet Shoes, 187
Very Nearly, 131

W
Wanderer's Song, A, 116
When Mother Reads Aloud, 88
Whether the Weather Be Fine, 174
Who Has Seen the Wind?, 181
Whole Duty of Children, 55
Wind, The, 182
Windy Nights, 180
World, The, 156
Wrong Start, The, 10
Wynken, Blynken, and Nod, 213

INDEX OF FIRST LINES

A

A child should always say what's
true, 55
A flea and a fly in a flue, 75
All things bright and beautiful,
160
Alone in the night on a dark hill,
203
An emerald is as green as grass,
164
An epicure, dining at Crewe, 52
Animal crackers, and cocoa to
drink, 44
A peanut sat on a railroad track,
53
As from the house your mother
sees, 87
As I walked by myself, 4
As I was standing in the street, 77
As long as I live, 5
At evening when the lamp is lit,
90
A tutor who tooted the flute, 73
A wind's in the heart of me, a fire's
in my heels, 116

B

Beautiful Soup, so rich and green,
47
Be present at our table, Lord, 50
Betty Botter bought some butter,
51
Between the bookcase and the
wall, 107

C

Can a little child like me, 218

D

Don't shirk, 60

E

Ere the moon begins to rise, 223
Everyone grumbled. The sky was
gray, 15

F

Four ducks on a pond, 145
From Ghoulies and Ghosties, 124
Fuzzy Wuzzy was a bear, 76

G

Girls and boys, come out to play,
22
Glory be to God for dappled
things—, 162
God, make my life a little light,
221
God be in my head, and in my
understanding, 219
God is so good that He will hear,
217
God watches o'er us all the day,
217
"Good morning, Merry Sunshine,"
191
Goodnight! Goodnight!, 220
Great, wide, beautiful, wonderful
World, 156

H

Happened that the moon was up
before I went to bed, 197
Have you ever heard of the
Sugarplum Tree?, 211
He clasps the crag with crooked
hands, 144
He thought he saw an Elephant,
80
Higglety, pigglety, pop!, 78
Hold fast to dreams, 68

How beautiful is the rain!, 183
How do you like to go up in a swing, 40
How much wood would a woodchuck chuck, 76
Hush, little baby, don't say a word, 225

I
I am the cat of cats. I am, 149
I eat my peas with honey, 53
If I can stop one Heart from breaking, 65
If I had a hundred dollars to spend, 140
If people ask me, 59
If woolly fleeces spread the heavenly way, 176
If you can keep your head when all about you, 66
If you see a fairy ring, 134
I got up this morning and meant to be good, 10
I have a little shadow that goes in and out with me, 7
I have an uncle I don't like, 19
I know a funny little man, 11
I know a little cupboard, 46
I like it when it's mizzly, 179
I'm a lean dog, a keen dog, a wild dog, and lone, 153
I meant to do my work today—, 29
I'm glad the sky is painted blue, 158
I'm going out to clean the pasture spring, 23
I'm hiding, I'm hiding, 35
I'm nobody! Who are you?, 9
I must go down to the seas again, to the lonely sea and the sky, 110
I must not throw upon the floor, 49
I never quite saw fairyfolk, 131
I never saw a moor, 61
I never saw a Purple Cow, 77

In jumping and tumbling, 208
In winter I get up at night, 194
I once had a sweet little doll, dears, 41
I saw you toss the kites on high, 182
I see the moon, 201
I thank you, God, 219
I think that I shall never see, 169
It was six men of Indostan, 96
I wandered lonely as a cloud, 167
I will be the gladdest thing, 2

L
Lady Moon, Lady Moon, where are you roving?, 196
Let others share your toys, my son, 60
Let us walk in the white snow, 187
Life did not bring me silken gowns, 165
Life has loveliness to sell, 63
Little drops of water, 62
Little Orphant Annie's come to our house to stay, 126
Long before the postman comes, 190
Lullaby, oh, lullaby!, 226

M
Marcia and I went over the curve, 48
Mary had a little lamb, 147
Measure me, sky!, 3
Moon, so round and yellow, 199
Mother, I love you so, 14
Mud is very nice to feel, 37
My daddy said, "My son, my son," 83
My dolly would not play with me, 42
My heart leaps up when I behold, 186

N
No matter what we are and who, 84

O

Oh, I have slipped the surly bonds
of earth, 121
Once there was an elephant, 72
One, two, 27
One misty, moisty, morning, 193
Out where the handclasp's a little
stronger, 114

P

Peter Piper picked a peck of
pickled peppers, 51
Please be careful where you tread,
135
Pop bottles pop-bottles, 79

R

Rain, rain, go away, 175
Red sky at night, 176
Ring-a-ring of little boys, 25
"Rock-a-by, baby, up in the tree-
top!," 227
Rock-a-bye baby, in the treetop,
226

S

Sea Shell, Sea Shell, 171
See lightning is flashing, 185
She reads the paper, 13
Sing a song of sixpence, 26
Some hae meat, and canna eat, 50
Something is there, 125
Stand straight, 58
Star light, star bright, 201
Stars over snow, 195
Swan swam over the sea, 145
Swing, swing, 38

T

The angels are stooping, 224
The bawl of the steer, 112
The children were shouting
together, 24
The fog comes, 178
The friendly cow all red and
white, 146

The gingham dog and the calico
cat, 92
The Goops they lick their fingers,
54
The lightning and thunder, 184
The little cares that fretted me,
159
The moon has a face like the clock
in the hall, 200
The Owl and the Pussycat went to
sea, 94
The railroad track is miles away,
118
The rain is raining all around, 184
There is no frigate like a book, 86
There was a crooked man, 28
There was a little turtle, 143
There was an Old Man with a
beard, 73
There was an old woman tossed
up in a basket, 130
There was a young lady named
Bright, 74
There was a young lady of Lynn,
52
The sea! The sea! The open sea!,
170
The stars are too many to count,
202
The world is so full of a number of
things, 220
The year's at the spring, 192
They say that God lives very
high!, 216
This little piggy went to market,
28
Three little kittens lost their
mittens, 150
Three of us afloat in the meadow
by the swing, 109
Tiger! Tiger! burning bright, 141
'Tis the gift to be simple, 64
To see a World in a grain of sand,
106
'Twas brillig, and the slithy toves,
70

Twinkle, twinkle, little star, 204
Two roads diverged in a yellow
  wood, 119

U
Until I saw the sea, 172
Up the airy mountain, 132

W
We built a ship upon the stairs, 30
Whatever brawls disturb the
  street, 18
What is pink? A rose is pink, 163
What is poetry? Who knows?, v
Whenever the moon and stars are
  set, 180
When in danger, 60
When Mother reads aloud, the
  past, 88

When my birthday was coming,
  17
When my brother Tommy, 16
When the night is cloudy, 136
When the voices of children are
  heard on the green, 209
When the wind is in the East,
  175
Where the pools are bright and
  deep, 31
Whether the weather be fine,
  174
White sheep, white sheep, 177
Who has seen the wind?, 181
"Will you walk into my parlor?"
  said the Spider to the Fly, 99
With lifted feet, hands still, 33
Wynken, Blynken, and Nod one
  night, 213